W9-BTF-655

Prairie Dogs

*written and photographed
by Frank Staub*

Lerner Publications Company • Minneapolis, Minnesota

For my Aunt Mary

Acknowledgments: Arizona Sonora Desert Museum, National Park Service, National Forest Service, National Wildlife Service, Texas State Parks, Kathleen Loften, and a special thanks to Paula Martin of the Prairie Ecosystem Conservation Alliance.

The photographs in this book were taken at: Arizona Sonora Desert Museum, Devils Tower National Monument, Fort Niobrara National Wildlife Refuge, Mackenzie State Park, Pawnee National Grasslands, Wichita Mountains National Wildlife Refuge, and Yellowstone National Park.

Additional photographs are reproduced by permission of: © Alan & Sandy Carey, pp. 30, 34, 38; © Wendy Shattil/Bob Rozinski, p. 8.

Thanks to our series consultant, Sharyn Fenwick, elementary science/math specialist. Mrs. Fenwick was the winner of the National Science Teachers Association 1991 Distinguished Teaching Award. She also was the recipient of the Presidential Award for Excellence in Math and Science Teaching, representing the state of Minnesota at the elementary level in 1992.

Early Bird Nature Books were conceptualized by Ruth Berman and designed by Steve Foley. Series editor is Joelle Goldman.

Copyright © 1998 by Lerner Publications Company

Website address: www.lernerbooks.com

Library of Congress Cataloging-in-Publication Data

Staub, Frank J.
    Prairie dogs / text and photographs by Frank Staub.
       p. cm. — (Early bird nature books)
    Includes index.
    Summary: An introduction to the physical characteristics, habits, and natural environment of the prairie dog.
    ISBN 0-8225-3038-4 (alk. Paper)
    1. Prairie dogs—Juvenile literature. [1. Prairie dogs.]
I. Title. II. Series.
QL737.R68S725 1998
599.36'7—dc21   97-48260

Manufactured in the United States of America
1 2 3 4 5 6 – JR – 03 02 01 00 99 98

Contents

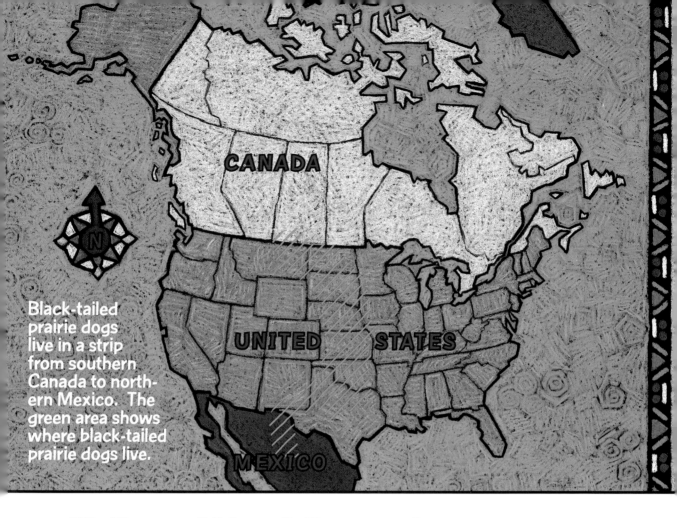

Black-tailed prairie dogs live in a strip from southern Canada to northern Mexico. The green area shows where black-tailed prairie dogs live.

CANADA

UNITED STATES

MEXICO

Be a Word Detective

Can you find these words as you read about the prairie dog's life? Be a detective and try to figure out what they mean. You can turn to the glossary on page 46 for help.

burrows	**nurse**	**refuges**
coteries	**prairie**	**rodents**
groom	**predators**	**territory**
kiss	**pups**	**town**

5

Chapter 1

The black-tailed prairie dog's scientific name is Cynomys ludovicianus. *What animal is the prairie dog related to?*

Barking Squirrels

Prairie dogs act much like puppies. They wag their tails. They make yipping sounds called barks. And when they sit up, they look like dogs begging for treats. But prairie dogs aren't dogs. Prairie dogs are related to squirrels.

Squirrels and prairie dogs are rodents. Rodents are animals that have long, sharp front teeth. Rodents use their teeth for cutting and biting. Mice, beavers, and woodchucks are rodents, too.

Prairie dogs eat all parts of a plant. They eat the stem, flowers, leaves, and roots.

Prairie dogs are small animals. They are about 1 foot long. And they weigh 2 to 3 pounds. They have short, strong legs and long, sharp claws.

There are two main kinds of prairie dogs. Both kinds have tan fur. But the white-tailed prairie dog has a white or gray tip on its tail. And the black-tailed prairie dog has a black tip on its tail.

There are many more black-tailed prairie dogs than white-tailed prairie dogs. This is a white-tailed prairie dog.

This prairie is in the state of Wyoming.

All prairie dogs live in North America. Most white-tailed prairie dogs live in the Rocky Mountains. Black-tailed prairie dogs live on the prairies. A prairie is a big grassy area where few trees grow.

Prairie dogs eat mostly plants. Prairie dogs eat the plants around their homes. Sometimes they eat most of the plants near their homes. If this happens, the prairie dogs may move to a new place.

Black-tailed prairie dogs get most of their water by eating juicy plants.

By the end of fall, a prairie dog may be so fat it is shaped like a pear.

Prairie dogs eat a lot in the spring, summer, and fall. By the end of fall, they are fat. They need to get fat to survive the winter. In winter, there aren't many plants to eat. The prairie dog's body uses its fat for food.

Chapter 2

Prairie dog homes are underground. What are prairie dogs' homes called?

An Underground Home

Black-tailed prairie dogs live under the ground. Their homes are holes called burrows (BUR-ohz). Usually more than one prairie dog lives in each burrow. Burrows protect prairie dogs from the heat of summer and the cold of winter.

Prairie dog burrows are made up of tunnels. The tunnels are just wide enough for a prairie dog to fit through. Some burrows have only one tunnel. Other burrows have several tunnels that are connected. Tunnels can go off in any direction. A burrow with many tunnels may be as long and deep as a big swimming pool.

Prairie dog burrows are only a few inches wide.

This prairie dog is beginning to dig its burrow.

Prairie dogs use their claws to dig burrows. Sometimes there are plant roots where prairie dogs dig. Then the prairie dogs use their teeth to bite through the roots.

Digging a burrow is a big job. Prairie dogs work together to dig a burrow. They start by digging a hole. The hole will be an entrance to the burrow. The prairie dogs keep digging deeper. As the tunnel gets deeper, the prairie dogs push dirt out of it. The dirt piles up in a mound around the entrance. Sometimes the mound is steep like a volcano.

A burrow mound may be 1 or 2 feet high. It helps to keep water out of the burrow.

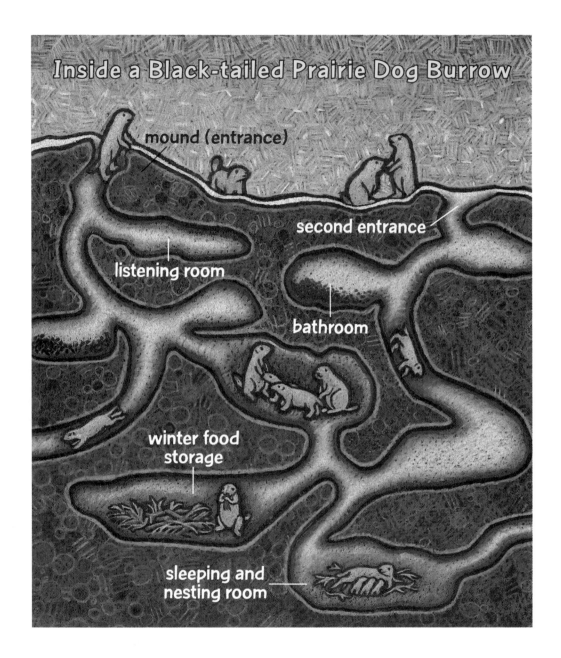

Inside a Black-tailed Prairie Dog Burrow

mound (entrance)

second entrance

listening room

bathroom

winter food storage

sleeping and nesting room

The prairie dogs dig deeper. They dig wide spaces to the sides of the tunnel. These spaces are like small rooms. There is a listening room. It is near the entrance. Some of the other rooms are sleeping rooms and bathrooms. They are deeper in the tunnel.

When a tunnel is nearly finished, prairie dogs will usually begin to dig upward. They dig until the tunnel opens above ground. Then the burrow has two entrances. The prairie dogs can come and go either way.

Some burrows are small and shallow and have only a few rooms. Others are big and deep and have many rooms.

Chapter 3

Prairie dogs live together in groups. What are these groups called?

Around Town

Black-tailed prairie dogs live in coteries (KOH-tuh-reez). Coteries are groups of prairie dogs who live together. The prairie dogs in each coterie are like a family. Most coteries

have five to ten prairie dogs. Some coteries
have more. Usually there is one adult male
and three or four adult females. The rest of the
members of the coterie are young.

A large coterie may have many burrows.

Kissing and grooming help prairie dogs get to know each other.

Prairie dogs eat, play, and lie in the sun with other members of their coterie. When prairie dogs from the same coterie meet, they kiss. Kissing is when prairie dogs touch mouth

20

to mouth. The prairie dogs may also groom each other. They groom by running their paws through each other's fur. Grooming keeps the prairie dogs' fur clean.

If two prairie dogs don't recognize one another, they will crawl closer. They smell and kiss one another.

Each coterie has its own territory, or neighborhood. Sometimes many territories are close together. A prairie dog usually stays in its own territory. But sometimes a prairie dog visits another territory. If the visitor sees a prairie dog from the other territory, the visitor usually runs home. Or the prairie dog who lives in the territory chases the visitor away. If the visitor does not leave, the two prairie dogs may fight.

One of these prairie dogs may be out of its territory.

Many years ago, prairie dog towns were huge. One man said he saw a town in Texas where millions of prairie dogs lived.

Areas with many territories are called towns. A small prairie dog town may be less than half a mile across. It may have a few hundred prairie dogs. A large town may be several miles across. Thousands of prairie dogs may live there.

Chapter 4

This prairie dog looks like it is dragging grass to its burrow. What might the grass be used for?

Raising a Family

Early in the spring, female black-tailed prairie dogs get ready to have babies. Each female builds a nest in her sleeping room. The nest is where the baby prairie dogs will be born. The female fills the nest with dry grass. The grass will keep her babies warm.

Prairie dogs have three to five babies at one time. The babies are called pups. Newborn pups are only 3 inches long. The pups have no hair. Their eyes are closed.

Newborn pups are helpless. But their mother takes good care of them. The pups nurse, or drink their mother's milk.

This pup is still too young to have much hair.

Pups usually don't go far from their burrows.

At first, the pups stay in the nest. When they are two or three weeks old, they start to grow fur. When they are five weeks old, their eyes open. The pups crawl around in the tunnels near their nest. When they are six or seven weeks old, they go outside their burrow for the first time.

At first the pups stay near their burrow. But soon they start exploring their coterie's territory. They begin nibbling on plants. Within the next few months, the prairie dogs stop nursing.

The adult prairie dogs in the coterie play with the pups. The pups watch the adults. By watching the adults, each pup learns how to kiss, groom, and find food.

When pups aren't eating or sleeping, they're usually playing.

This pup is learning how to groom another prairie dog's fur.

Pups sometimes visit other territories. The adults in other territories do not chase the pups away. But by the end of the summer, young prairie dogs are nearly grown. Then if they visit another territory, they are chased away.

In the fall, most of the young males move out of their coteries. They start coteries of their own. They may move into empty burrows. Or they may dig new burrows.

A female prairie dog usually stays in the same coterie all her life. But sometimes food is hard to find. If there is not enough food for the coterie, young females may leave. They join other coteries that have enough food.

Both males and females may leave their coterie. But they rarely leave their home town.

Chapter 5

Coyotes hunt prairie dogs. What are animals who hunt other animals called?

Enemies of Prairie Dogs

Many animals hunt black-tailed prairie dogs. Animals who hunt other animals for food are called predators (PRED-uh-turz). Coyotes (kye-OH-teez), black-footed ferrets, and hawks are some of the predators who hunt prairie dogs.

These prairie dogs are looking out for danger.

Prairie dogs are always watching for predators. Often, prairie dogs stand on top of their burrow mounds. They look all around for predators. Prairie dogs eat the plants near their burrows. So these plants stay short. This way the prairie dogs can see far.

If a predator comes near, the first prairie dog to see it barks in a high voice. The barking warns other prairie dogs. The other prairie dogs stand still and listen. If the prairie dog barks again, the others dash for their burrows. Prairie dogs are usually safe in their burrows. Most predators cannot follow a prairie dog into its burrow. The predators are too big.

Few predators could fit inside this hole.

A prairie dog's eyes are near the top of its head. So it doesn't have to come far out of its burrow to look around.

When a prairie dog runs into its burrow, it usually stops in the room just below the entrance. It listens for danger. When it thinks the predator is gone, the prairie dog creeps up to the entrance. It looks around to make sure the predator is gone.

Snakes and ferrets are very thin predators.
They can fit easily into a prairie dog burrow.
That's why most burrows have two entrances.

Prairie rattlesnakes are one of many prairie dog predators.

If a predator comes in one entrance, the prairie dog may be able to escape through the other entrance.

Prairie dogs make hundreds of different kinds of calls. This prairie dog is making the "all clear" call.

Chapter 6

Cattle and prairie dogs often live on the same land. They eat the same grass. What problem has this caused for prairie dogs?

The Prairie's Friend

Once there were over a hundred million black-tailed prairie dogs. Many of them dug their burrows on ranches. Ranches are large farms where people keep cattle. The prairie dogs ate some of the grass on the ranches. But ranchers wanted all the grass for their cattle. So ranchers killed many prairie dogs. About 2 million prairie dogs are left.

Cities have also caused problems for prairie dogs. People built cities on the prairie. So prairie dogs have less room to dig their burrows.

Prairie dogs need open land to live on.

Black-footed ferrets hunt prairie dogs for food. The ferrets can't survive without prairie dogs.

If there are few prairie dogs, it's harder for other animals to live on the prairie. Many predators eat prairie dogs. The black-footed ferret eats mostly prairie dogs. After ranchers killed most of the prairie dogs, almost all the black-footed ferrets died.

Prairie dogs dig good homes. If prairie dogs move out of their burrows, other animals may move in. Snakes, burrowing owls, turtles, and black-footed ferrets may move into old prairie dog burrows.

Burrowing owls only live in empty prairie dog burrows.

Prairie dogs also help plants grow on the prairie. As prairie dogs eat plants, new plants can grow. The new plants are strong and healthy. Strong plants make good food for animals who live on the prairie.

The American bison takes dust baths by rolling on prairie dog mounds. Dust baths help bison get rid of biting insects.

Prairie dogs stir up the soil where they dig. This helps plants grow around a prairie dog's burrow.

Some people still kill prairie dogs. But other people have helped prairie dogs. They set aside refuges (REF-yoo-jehz) for prairie dogs. A refuge is a safe place for animals to live.

Some prairie dogs live close to people and their roads.

Most prairie dogs live far from cities. But you can see prairie dog towns in refuges. And sometimes you might see prairie dog burrows beside highways and railroads.

42

It's fun to watch prairie dogs. They kiss. They play. They live in towns. In some ways they're just like us.

Prairie dogs are important. They help other animals and plants live on the prairie.

On Sharing a Book

As you know, adults greatly influence a child's attitude toward reading. When a child sees you read, or when you share a book with a child, you're sending a message that reading is important. Show the child that reading a book together is important to you. Find a comfortable, quiet place. Turn off the television and limit other distractions, such as telephone calls.

Be prepared to start slowly. Take turns reading parts of this book. Stop and talk about what you're reading. Talk about the photographs. You may find that much of the shared time is spent discussing just a few pages. This discussion time is valuable for both of you, so don't move through the book too quickly. If the child begins to lose interest, stop reading. Continue sharing the book at another time. When you do pick up the book again, be sure to revisit the parts you have already read. Most importantly, enjoy the book!

Be a Vocabulary Detective

You will find a word list on page 5. Words selected for this list are important to the understanding of the topic of this book. Encourage the child to be a word detective and search for the words as you read the book together. Talk about what the words mean and how they are used in the sentence. Do any of these words have more than one meaning? You will find these words defined in a glossary on page 46.

What about Questions?

Use questions to make sure the child understands the information in this book. Here are some suggestions:

What did this paragraph tell us? What does this picture show? What do you think we'll learn about next? What does a prairie look like? Why do prairie dogs live under the ground? What are the parts of a prairie dog burrow? How are prairie dog coteries like people's neighborhoods? How is eating all the grass around their burrows helpful to prairie dogs? What dangers must prairie dogs watch out for? How do prairie dogs help other animals live on the prairie? What is your favorite part of this book? Why?

If the child has questions, don't hesitate to respond with questions of your own such as: What do *you* think? Why? What is it that you don't know? If the child can't remember certain facts, turn to the index.

Introducing the Index

The index is an important learning tool. It helps readers get information quickly without searching throughout the whole book. Turn to the index on page 48. Choose an entry, such as food, and ask the child to use the index to find out what prairie dogs eat. Repeat this exercise with as many entries as you like. Ask the child to point out the differences between an index and a glossary. (The index helps readers find information quickly, while the glossary tells readers what words mean.)

All the World in Metric!

Although our monetary system is in metric units (based on multiples of 10), the United States is one of the few countries in the world that does not use the metric system of measurement. Here are some conversion activities you and the child can do using a calculator:

WHEN YOU KNOW:	MULTIPLY BY:	TO FIND:
miles	1.609	kilometers
feet	0.3048	meters
inches	2.54	centimeters
gallons	3.787	liters
pounds	0.454	kilograms

Activities

Make up a story about a prairie dog coterie. What would a day in the life of the members of the coterie be like? Be sure to include information from this book.

Visit a zoo to see prairie dogs and other rodents. How are prairie dogs similar to other rodents in the zoo? How are they different?

Draw a picture of a prairie dog town. Show the different coteries in the town. Show the different burrows in the coteries.

Glossary

burrows (BUR-ohz)—the holes prairie dogs live in

coteries (KOH-tuh-reez)—groups of prairie dogs who live together

groom—to use claws or teeth to clean fur

kiss—when prairie dogs touch mouth to mouth

nurse—to drink mother's milk

prairie—a large area of grassy land with few trees

predators (PREH-duh-turz)—animals who hunt and eat other animals

pups—baby prairie dogs

refuges (REF-yoo-jehz)—safe places to live

rodents—animals with large, sharp front teeth for chewing

territory—a prairie dog's neighborhood

town—a group of prairie dog neighborhoods

Index

Pages listed in **bold** type refer to photographs.